BODY CARE™

cherish your body as a temple.

Learn to honor your extraordinary body
as a living temple and listen to the healing messages she whispers.

BODY CARE COPYRIGHT

Copyright © 2010-2013 by Miranda J. Barrett.
Original Concept Copyright © 2008 by Miranda J. Barrett.
Copyright © 2010 Front Cover Artwork by Helena Nelson-Reed.

All rights reserved. This book may not be reproduced in whole or in part without written permission. In accordance with the U.S. Copyright act of 1976, the scanning, uploading and electronic sharing of any part of this book without permission of the publisher is unlawful piracy and theft of the author's intellectual property.

If you would like to use material from the book (other than for review purposes), prior written permission must be obtained by contacting either the publisher at:

Info@ MirandaJBarrett.com
or the artist at www.HelenaNelsonReed.com
Thank you for the support of the author and the artist's rights.

Please note:

The written or spoken information, ideas, procedures and suggestions contained and presented in 'BODY CARE' workshops and books are meant for educational purposes only and are not for diagnosis. It should not be used as a substitute for your physician's advice. 'BODY CARE' is not therapy, and is not intended to replace the recommendations of a licensed health practitioner. It is the responsibility of the reader to consult with his or her own medical Doctor, Counselor, Therapist or other competent professional regarding any condition before adopting any suggestion in this book.

BODY CARE™

Dedicated to the self-care of the miraculous physical temple and to the wisdom to treat the body as a sacred altar for our essence.

MISSION STATEMENT

To guide and facilitate women
in becoming their most beautiful and radiant selves.

To acknowledge and embrace the well of love
and power which lies within all women and to ignite the
awakening and embodying of this life force.

To empower each woman, through exquisite self-care and love,
to live her fullest life possible, and to walk her path of wisdom
and truth, as she shares this light and knowledge
with all beings.

IN DEEP GRATITUDE

Thank you

The creation, birth and life of 'A Woman's Truth' would not have been possible without the love, support and devotion from the following angels in my life:

My beautiful daughter Megan who naturally embodies the teachings of living in her truth and integrity, thank you for the creative gift of the beautiful artwork. Helena Nelson-Reed for her generosity of spirit in allowing her extraordinary artwork, which embodies the teachings so magnificently, to grace the covers. Dennise Marie Keller for her unwavering support and dedication to the teachings and for proofing, editing, aligning and translating my vision into the technical world of manifestation. Dan Fowler for his creative genius and dedication. Lucy Alexander and Suzanne Ryan, my dearest friends for their amazing editing and wholehearted encouragement. Monica Marsh for her commitment, support and belief in the workshops. Maggie Crawford, my mum, for her proofing and for being a living example of the teachings. Cait Myer and Katie Steen for their patience and ability to decipher my handwriting and for formatting the books. Bethany Kelly for her support. Deborah Waring for holding the space for the conception of 'A Woman's Truth' to be born and for her insight in the first year of teaching and Emmanuel for believing in my vision.

My mentors and teachers Rod Stryker, Adyashanti and Alison Armstrong, Max Simon and Jeffrey Van Dyk for their continuous and guiding light in my life, their never-ending belief in my potential and for always teaching me the way to evolve into my highest and most potent self. And to all of you beautiful and courageous women who are committing to living your truth and transforming into your most radiant selves,

thank you.

A PRELUDE
An overture to self-care.

Body Care is Miranda's gift to the reader and the reader's gift to herself. The daily practices in this book will show you how to love and honor yourself on every level. It navigates the reader through daily reflections of awareness, self-care, empowerment and healing. It helps the reader tune into the natural frequencies and resonance of her body. It delves into the practical and the sensual, capturing the essence of the feminine body and the feminine soul and reflecting it back to the reader.

Miranda's genius is that she is able to present very meaningful material in a very easy to read and easy to use manner. In Body Care, Miranda has created a daily friend that guides the reader on an exploration of all aspects of her body, including some that are often not considered. It helps the reader lovingly care for her whole self, in health as well as illness. Nothing Miranda suggests is costly, complicated, or time consuming. It is for everyone and every lifestyle. If followed page-by-page this book will profoundly affect the reader throughout her lifetime.

Miranda's mission is for all of us to live a spirited, self-aware life. She has dedicated herself to raising consciousness by showing individuals how to reclaim health in all aspects of their being. Body Care brings together Miranda's unique wisdom and impressive knowledge. Her book will be a source of transformation and light in many people's lives.

~ **Benjamin Shield, Ph.D.**
Rolfer and author of 'Healers on Healing', 'For the Love of God',
'Handbook for the Soul', and 'Handbook for the Heart'.

Some people call me a Beauty Guru. I have spent decades in a career in an industry that some uses to prey on the weak and the insecure, but with an award from the Queen of England for services to the cosmetics industry, it lead me on a road to challenge the very business that feeds my children. I have literally spent a lifetime trying to sideline the train of thought and practice of demeaning women to replace it with the championing of the inner beauty and most importantly to celebrate the diversity of women.

I am a short, slightly rotund, well-endowed woman that speaks from her heart, shoots from her hip and adores the female form in any size, color and proportion. There are limited amounts of changes you can make to your exterior, and most would require an artful practitioner (surgeon) to assist. Nevertheless, as I age and grow more comfortable and confident about myself from the outside, I seek advice and inspiration in altering my body from within. This is something only I can do. This is where Miranda comes in with her experience, wisdom and compassion and guides the female form to an achievable and attainable vision. A vision emerges of a simple self, not glorified or unrealistic and one that only you can do.

Miranda and I met when her brother married my best friend, and as we grew as a somewhat unconventional family, we discovered a kinship beyond the marriage of our loved ones. We discovered self. A woman's right to cherish her body inside and out. The book you are about to read embodies Miranda (no pun intended) and brings to the forefront what you can do to better your life, your body, your health.

I applaud Miranda's chutzpah. She is an oracle of confidence and self-worth.

~ Millie Kendall, MBE.
Beauty Brand Creator

BODY CARE™
Gems of Love

BODY CARE 1

GRATITUDE FOR THE BODY 2

MIND, BODY AND WILL 3

LISTENING TO THE BODY 5

THE FOUNDATIONAL TRINITY 6

CARING FOR THE BODY 8

ADORNING THE BODY 10

BODY SYMBOLOGY 12

THE SKIN 20

MAKEUP 29

INTERNAL CLEANSING 30

HONORING MENSTRUATION 34

BREAST AND FEMININE CARE 39

THE HAIR 41

HAIR REMOVAL 43

THE EYES 45

THE EARS	47
THE NOSE	48
THE TEETH	50
THE JAW	53
THE TONGUE	55
THE THROAT AND NECK	56
THE HANDS	57
THE FEET	59
THE BODY AND THE ENVIRONMENT	62
COOKWARE	67
TRAVEL	68
REVEAL MORE TRUTH	71
CHARTS, CHARTS, GLORIOUS CHARTS	73
EXQUISITE SELF-CARE CHART	74

Download a copy of **Exquisite Self-Care Chart**

from Miranda's website at:

www.MirandaJBarrett.com/resources/body-care

A DAILY PRACTICE
commit to yourself

*F*ollow these simple steps daily as a way to instill and strengthen your heartfelt resolve to love yourself. This will help to keep you aligned, transforming and on track, giving you a stable foundation for the rest of your life. As a gift to yourself, please mark the teachings as you read them through and congratulate yourself with each one. See each day as a commitment to take exquisite care of yourself.

- ◊ DAY ONE: BODY CARE 1
- ◊ DAY TWO: GRATITUDE FOR THE BODY 2
- ◊ DAY THREE: MIND, BODY AND WILL 3
- ◊ DAY FOUR: LISTENING TO THE BODY 5
- ◊ DAY FOUR: THE FOUNDATIONAL TRINITY 6
- ◊ DAY FIVE: CARING FOR THE BODY 8
- ◊ DAY SIX: ADORNING THE BODY 10
- ◊ DAY SEVEN: BODY SYMBOLOGY 12
- ◊ DAY EIGHT: THE SKIN 20
- ◊ DAY NINE: MAKEUP 29
- ◊ DAY TEN: INTERNAL CLEANSING 30
- ◊ DAY ELEVEN: HONORING MENSTRUATION 34
- ◊ DAY TWELVE: BREAST AND FEMININE CARE 39
- ◊ DAY THIRTEEN: THE HAIR 41
- ◊ DAY FOURTEEN: HAIR REMOVAL 43

- DAY FIFTEEN: THE EYES 45
- DAY SIXTEEN: THE EARS 47
- DAY SEVENTEEN: THE NOSE 48
- DAY EIGHTEEN: THE TEETH 50
- DAY NINTEEN: THE JAW 53
- DAY TWENTY: THE TONGUE 55
- DAY TWENTY-ONE: THE THROAT AND NECK 56
- DAY TWENTY-TWO: THE HANDS 57
- DAY TWENTY-THREE: THE FEET 59
- DAY TWENTY-FOUR: THE BODY AND THE ENVIRONMENT 62
- DAY TWENTY-FIVE: COOKWARE 67
- DAY TWENTY-SIX: TRAVEL 68
- DAY TWENTY-SEVEN: REVEAL MORE TRUTH 71
- EVERYDAY: CHARTS, CHARTS, GLORIOUS CHARTS 73
- EVERYDAY: EXQUISITE SELF-CARE CHART 74

Download a copy of **Exquisite Self-Care Chart**

from Miranda's website at:

www.MirandaJBarrett.com/resources/body-care

A LIFE WORTH LIVING

*"Never give from your well.
Always give from your overflow."*
~ Rumi

All too often as women, your own needs are denied for the benefit of others as you orchestrate your life through demands and expectations you feel responsible for. Unfortunately, this can leave you without the juice and energy needed to be present fully and to enjoy life. During these readings, you will continually discover more about who you truly are and learn the tools needed to live your most authentic and fulfilling life possible. From this place, you will experience being 'full to overflowing' and all the joy and energy this brings.

As you delve into these teachings, you will explore, laugh, study, share, and freely express who you are. In this sacred space, you will ultimately learn your truth as a woman in order to shine, to embody your own beauty, believe in your own worth, and take exquisite care of yourself. For only in this way can you truly be of service.

During these guidebooks, many of the basic needs of women will be explored such as sleep, nutrition, creativity, movement and time to replenish. A topic has been chosen for each book and a cohesive and practical foundation is laid out to inspire and guide you. This will bring about a new strength and resolve which will allow your needs to become a priority, without letting your outer world dictate otherwise. By the end of our time together, the concept of being confident, loving, serene and passionate will no longer be a distant fantasy. Instead, these and many other extraordinary qualities that you naturally embody as a woman will flow with ease, grace and love.

With life's demands so high, it has become imperative that your needs are first acknowledged, honored and then taken care of. From this vantage point, your relationship with yourself then has the potential to be transformed into one of self-love. The beauty is this in turn creates a life that not only fulfills you and your life's purpose, but also allows everyone touched by your presence to receive this gift.

I look forward to spending this precious time with you.

Welcome to A Woman's Truth.

Sincerely and with love,

Miranda

BODY CARE
The body is your temple.

The body is the vessel, which houses where you live. Without the body, you have no home and no way to express yourself. In certain spiritual traditions, it is said that souls line up to incarnate as human beings, because being human is such a sought-after experience. When you are having a tough day you may well question why, yet the physical experience of having a body means that you are given the gift of the senses. You get to taste, to see, to hear, to smell, to hold and to feel. Sometimes these sensations can cause divine pleasure and other times extreme pain, yet this is the experience and miracle of being born into the physical body.

As part of your life experience is to feel the sensations of the body and the world around you, it makes sense to honor the world closest to you, your physical form. By taking exquisite care of this extraordinary machine, it will respond beautifully. When the body is rested, nourished, hydrated and stretched it seems to shine with vitality. When you listen and pay attention to its basic needs, it responds by being an athlete, a workhorse, a sensual being, a creator, loving arms and even a shoulder on which to cry.

Your duty, as your body's keeper, is to take good care of its fundamental needs. The payment is small in comparison to the pay-off. Just look at any great athlete or musician performing. With attention, training and learning how to respond to its needs, your body will perform miracles for you repeatedly.

"We are born with one body.
If we do not treat that body with love and respect it will die,
and then we will have nowhere to live."

~Quote

GRATITUDE FOR THE BODY
Give thanks daily.

When was the last time you thanked your body for meeting all the demands you make on it? Did you notice all the times when you were exhausted and yet managed to push through the task anyway? It was your body that kept you going and went the extra mile. Yet there will be occasions where you will push too far and refuse to listen to the many cries of the body. In reality these are crimes against yourself and if ignored can lead to harm. Instead, the next time you are thirsty, make it a priority to find a drink; when you cannot even keep your eyes open, find a place to lie down and close them.

"There have been times when I am driving late at night, and my eyes become heavy. It is though someone is placing weights on them and it is all I can do to keep them open. In that moment, my body is telling me that it no longer has energy to be driving a lethal weapon. Yet, instead of stopping and resting, which would be listening to my body, I drink some water, crank up the radio and open the window, forcing myself to stay awake and complete the demand at hand. Then, when I arrive safely at my destination, do I stop to thank my body for taking care of me and pushing through the exhaustion? Chances are, had someone else been driving, I would thank them profusely, ask them if they are ok or if they need a glass of water? Yet often I ignore my own needs. I may stop to pee if desperate, but this is a far cry from honoring and really listening to me."
~ Miranda

With this in mind, next time your body accomplishes the impossible for you, thank it. Each night as you fall asleep, take a moment to drop into a sense of gratitude for how this miraculous and well-oiled machine performed for you. Moreover, when it does talk to you, such as when you suffer from a headache or a cold, instead of being annoyed, realize this is your body's way of saying enough is enough. Just as you would put a cranky child to bed at that time, listen to your body. Listen to the extraordinary and miraculously designed form that you take for granted.

Treat this vessel with love, respect and gratitude,
otherwise it may collapse before its time.

MIND, BODY AND WILL
An abundance of partnership.

You are not just a body nor are you just your mind, your emotions or your Higher Self. You are in fact in relationship with all these aspects of yourself. It seems as though the problems start when you override one for extended periods of time, without checking to see if the rest of the team is on board.

No one likes a dictator. There may be situations when one aspect will bulldoze through another. Have you ever noticed when you are deep in an emotional wound, that you have no desire for food? It is as though you are drowning in so much emotion that the physical form cannot tolerate taking anything else in. As long as this is temporary, you will survive. However, if the emotions overwhelm you for too long, then it may be necessary for an outside influence to step in and remind you that you need to eat something. At this point, honoring the physical as well as the emotional body is vital.

The mind, like the emotions, may also dictate and ignore the body's needs. It is important to remember that the body never lies and that it has its own intelligence. Pain, exhaustion, difficulty breathing are all sure signs that you need to pay attention and to change what you are doing, even if your mind is demanding you to carry on.

"My father suffered from multiple sclerosis, an illness that destroys the nervous system. My grandmother always told me that she felt the reason he became ill was that he over-forced his will. My father was an oarsman, rowing in national, televised races. In his last year, the oarsman in front of him got stage fright and collapsed in the beginning of the race. My father, to keep the boat from capsizing, rowed the rest of the race with one hand holding the collapsed man upright and still rowing with the other. An extraordinary feat you may think and amazingly, they only lost by one length. Yet, according to my grandmother, he collapsed after the race and was unable to move for about three weeks afterwards. Did his will override the ability of his already strong body? Did he actually damage his nervous system by pushing himself too far? We will never know." ~ Miranda

In certain situations, even spirituality can override and ignore the body's needs. Some meditation disciplines teach you not to move at all while meditating, even if your knees are hurting. Yet by sitting for so long, you may actually be damaging your knee joints. The point is to keep everything in balance and letting the Higher Self lead the way and making sure that you honor and listen to your body. It is all about balance.

"Sometimes your body is smarter than you are."
~Author Unknown

LISTENING TO THE BODY

If you listen to the whispers, you will not have to hear the cries.

The physical form is continuously communicating with you. Sometimes it screams, other times it whispers, yet when you actually stop to listen, it will let you know exactly what it needs and usually the need is relatively simple.

"I am tired, let me rest."
"I am thirsty, hydrate me."
"I am stiff, stretch me."
"I am full, stop feeding me."

The trouble begins when you ignore the subtle messages.

It is rather like driving a car. The check engine light comes on. You see the red light; you feel the stress and the tension it invokes in you, yet you choose to disregard it. Well of course, it is highly inconvenient and sometimes a part of you decides to keep ignoring the blatant message and gamble heading for home anyway. The point is, you never know exactly what damage you may be doing. Yes, you may get away with it, but you could also be destroying your whole engine. In addition, the difference between a car and a body is that you can buy a new car!

The point is, it can sometimes be annoying and tiresome when the body has a need or if it breaks down. However, if you always remember that it has its own intelligence and is designed to survive, you may be able to accept that it is a better choice to listen and honor the messages your body gives you. When given what it requires, the body can repair itself and reestablish a state of health for whatever is next. The human body will survive on very little given the test. Yet over time, life takes its toll and the quality of your existence diminishes should you continue down the path towards self-destruction, rather than the creation of health and well-being.

THE FOUNDATIONAL TRINITY

And in the beginning there was...

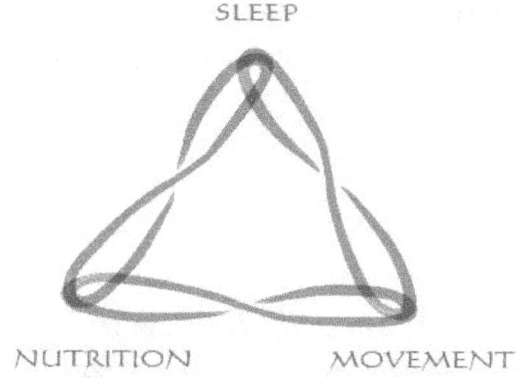

This is the basic foundation of self-care.

By investing in your relationship with sleep, movement and nutrition, you will be infused with these essential tools which not only supply you with life force, but also give you the energy to live the life you desire. By choosing *not* to honor this 'Foundational Trinity' of rest, movement and nourishment, you place your body into a state of stress and deny the reality of what you truly need. It makes sense that a lack of sleep, unbalanced food choices or a sedentary lifestyle will not properly prepare you or your body for a day of joyful living.

Living in today's world is stressful. Yet what is being offered here is a new way of being. Instead of succumbing to the pressure of stress, listen to your bodies' voice to inform you about how you are living your life and the choices you are making.

Do not ignore stress. It is an important messenger.

Pressure and tension are sure signs that a thought experience or belief you are having feels as though it is heading in the wrong direction. Stress is your physical, mental or emotional reaction to these situations, so you must pay close attention to these feelings.

Do not shy away from them, instead lean into their guidance and message. Pause for a moment, take a breath and bring yourself back into the present moment. Allow this stillness to balance you and from this grounded and centered place be open to the possibility that there may be another choice. It may be as simple as accepting what already is, as challenging as that may be. By claiming and fully living, the teachings of 'The Foundational Trinity' your life will change. This is the groundwork needed to support the rest of your life ahead.

*"Be careful what you water
your dreams with. Water them with worry and fear
and you will produce weeds that choke the life from your dream.
Water them with optimism and solutions and you will cultivate success.
Always be on the lookout for ways to turn a problem
into an opportunity for success.
Always be on the lookout for ways to nurture your dream."*
~ Lao Tzu

CARING FOR THE BODY

From the inside out.

The external parts of the body are very effective in telling you what is happening. If you bump into something, you get a bruise or a scrape. If your hands feel or look dirty, you wash them. Yet sometimes the internal world of the body is silently hurting. How would you know? The loving guideline here is maintenance.

Many daily routines you can follow will support the structure and systems of the body's internal organs. By consciously choosing to incorporate them into your life, the body will respond by keeping itself healthy. It just needs the right tools.

Ways To Care For The Body:

- Keep the body hydrated.
- Breathe full, long, deep breaths.
- Nourish the body with live, nutritious food.
- Eat enough fiber to keep the digestive system clean.
- Move the body by exercising and stretching.
- Sweat the body to remove toxins.
- Keep the spine strong and upright by core strengthening exercise.
- Do not force any part of the body to stay in one position too long.
- Practice kegal exercises daily to stimulate and strengthen the pelvic floor.
- Become aware of ongoing stress and find a conscious solution.
- Rest and relax the body as needed.
- Get regular blood work and check-ups with a doctor
- Pay attention to changes in your skin, weight and energy levels.

Much of this is in 'The Foundational Trinity.' Use this time to listen and then respond to whatever messages you are being sent.

It is no longer appropriate to ignore this temple called your body.

ADORNING THE BODY

*As you beautify your temple,
make sure you are still comfortable to kick off your heels.*

What you dress the physical body in is a direct expression of who you are. The color and the texture of the fabric, the jewelry, the shoes, the bag or the nails are all accessories, which can change how you feel. Pay attention to what else is going on.

Are you comfortable in what you are wearing?

If the wire in the bra is digging into your breast and your back hurts from the high heels, is it worth it? Perhaps it is more important to feel good rather than look good. What is being encouraged here is a combination of beauty and comfort.

WAYS TO CREATE BEAUTY AND COMFORT:

- **The quality of fabric is important.**
  Choose one that allows the skin to breathe.

- **The cut of the garment can make or break a look.**
  Find out what enhances all your best features. You know when you look good.

- Choose colors that match your natural skin tones and resonate with you.

- Choose attractive, comfortable shoes or slip off your heels under the table.

- If every time you wear wool, itchy rashes or hives appear, stop wearing wool. Your body is desperately trying to talk to you.

◆ Check for metal allergies when wearing jewelry.
   Pure gold is one of the cleanest metals.

◆ If you have been doing, doing, doing, change out of your practical clothes and put on something feminine, soft or silky.
   Notice how this changes your whole energy field.

◆ Scents, perfumes and essential oils can also beautifully enhance the feminine.

BODY SYMBOLOGY
Messages from the temple.

Just as there are many ways to diagnose disease, so there are many ways to interpret the direct messages you are receiving from your body every day.

Some messages are simple and obvious, such as bumping into things and hurting yourself. Perhaps this means your body is not grounded or you may be distracted and not paying attention. Other possibilities may be, you are tired or multi-tasking too much. Whatever the reason, the point of the message is to slow down, pay attention and become more aware of what is actually going on around you.

The bottom line is, wake up!

Yet other messages may be harder to discern. You may need to look deeper into unhealthy beliefs or behavior patterns, which may lead to injury or disease.

The First Question To Ask Here Is:

◆ **What are the stresses that keep reoccurring in your life?**

The brain is designed to deal with stress the best it can, yet after a while the tension can build to a point that the mind can no longer cope. At this moment, the brain decides to store the stress and sends a message to the part of the body that directly corresponds with the inflicting situation.

An example of this would be, if over a period of time, you were extremely fearful of not having enough money to cover your bills. When this message is repeated, eventually the brain can no longer deal with the stress. Therefore, in its infinite intelligence, the mind may choose to stimulate the production of fat as a way to protect you from possible starvation. Even though a lack of funds does not necessarily lead to a lack of food, in today's world, money does equal the ability to eat. Thus, the instinctual and biological reaction of the body in times of perceived famine is to store as much fat as possible. It makes perfect survival sense, because then you will live longer.

The trouble is that gaining weight in modern times is not going to help pay the rent or the bills. Therefore, it is important to listen to the message the stress is sending and then find another solution to relax the brain. It might be as simple as just reminding yourself you will not die if you cannot pay some bills or maybe it is about eliminating some of your expenses. Perhaps you even have to move, which would be thoroughly annoying, but the bottom line is you will still survive.

The following are some suggestions surrounding your body and the symbolic meaning behind a specific pain or illness. Just as you can use symbology in your dreams, it is also an extraordinary tool in your waking life.

You might also enjoy the messages of animals that cross your path in your daily life by receiving the symbolism they represent. Each animal has its own meaning, such as a butterfly being transformation, ant symbolizing patience, hummingbird embodying joy or territory, squirrel demonstrating gathering, lizard depicting dreaming and spider invoking creativity and weaving or a coyote being the trickster and hawk, the messenger. When these messengers come into your life, you must pay attention particularly if they appear to you more than once.

Remember, sometimes a cut is just a cut; diarrhea is simply caused by bad food and a headache by too much time on the computer or dehydration. Again, these are simple yet eloquent demands that the body needs attention to thrive.

If you are having a reoccurring symptom, spend a moment pondering what the message may be. If every time you are on vacation you become ill, maybe this is a sign you are exhausted. If, when you go and visit a certain family member you get an upset stomach, ask the question, what is it about that situation you cannot digest?

There is no right or wrong here.

It is more about going inward and following your own compass. By being quiet and still you can then listen to the subtle, yet powerful and life saving messages that your precious body is desperately trying to tell you.

The praying mantis is the perfect depiction of needing more stillness, peace, quiet and calm. If the mantis appears in your life it is a sure sign that your world has become flooded with so much business, activity or chaos that you can no longer hear the still small voice within you because of the external noise you have created.

"Many people can listen to their cat more intelligently than they can listen to their own despised body. Because they attend to their pet in a cherishing way, it returns their love. Their body, however, may have to let out an earth-shattering scream in order to be heard at all."
~Marion Woodman

BODY SYMBOLOGY
possible body part messages.

- **Ankles**
  Support and change of direction.

- **Arms and Legs**
  Strength, support, mobility and forward motion.

- **Back**
  Support and flexibility, lower back connects to financial support.

- **Bones**
  Structure, strength, alignment and support.

- **Breasts**
  Nurturing for yourself and others.

- **Buttocks**
  Power.

- **Ears**
  Ability or inability to listen or hear.

- **Eyes**
  Ability or inability to see.

- **Feet**
  Grounding, direction.

- **Hands**
  How life is handled, holding on too tight.

- **Hips**
  Balance and bearing the weight of creation.

- ◆ **Jaw**
  Where anger and resentment are held at bay.

- ◆ **Joints**
  Flexibility.

- ◆ **Knees**
  Lack of support, right knee symbolizes father, left knee mother.

- ◆ **Muscles**
  Ability to move.

- ◆ **Neck**
  Stress, flexibility and intuitive locking point.

- ◆ **Nose**
  Discernment and noticing the obvious.

- ◆ **Ribcage**
  Protection.

- ◆ **Shoulder**
  Bearing the weight of the world and relationships.

- ◆ **Skin**
  Protection, separation and individuality.

- ◆ **Sinuses**
  Irritation and space for new ideas.

- ◆ **Teeth and Gums**
  Conviction, resolution and protection.

- ◆ **Throat**
  Speaking your truth or holding denials.

- ◈ **Right Side of the Body**
  Masculine, doing and giving.

- ◈ **Left Side of the Body**
  Feminine, being and receiving.

Possible organ messages.

- ◈ **Heart**
  Seat of love, conviction, desire and depression.

- ◈ **Kidneys and Bladder**
  Seat of fear, territory, insecurity and irritation.

- ◈ **Liver**
  Seat of anger, resentment and bitterness.

- ◈ **Lungs**
  Seat of grief, inspiration and sadness.

- ◈ **Pancreas**
  Sweetness of life.

- ◈ **Stomach and Intestines**
  Digesting and assimilating life and receiving nourishment.

- ◈ **Spleen**
  Seat of worry and obsessing.

- ◈ **Womb**
  Source of creation and nurturing.

Possible body messages.

- **Aching**
  Longing to be loved and connection to spirituality.

- **Anxiety**
  Not trusting your intuition.

- **Body Odor**
  Disliking the self and keeping people away.

- **Breast Problems**
  Lack of self-nourishment and allowing others to suck you dry.

- **Breathing Problems**
  Not taking up space and the inability to take in life.

- **Canker Sores**
  Unspoken truths and denials.

- **Calluses**
  Hardened concepts and ideas.

- **Cellulite**
  Stored anger and self-punishment.

- **Circulation**
  Restraint and the ability to speak honestly.

- **Constipation**
  Lies, deceit, denials and stuck holding onto the past.

- **Cramps**
  Holding on.

◆ **Fat**
Stuffed emotions, protection, isolation and artificial power.

◆ **Headache**
Lack of confidence and not honoring yourself.

◆ **Hemorrhoids**
Holding onto the past and resistance to change.

◆ **Hives**
Intuitive warning.

◆ **Hunchback**
Carrying the burden of life and barricading the heart and feelings.

◆ **Stomach Upsets**
Indigestible situations, people and ideas.

◆ **Urinary-Tract Infection**
Pissed off and marking territory.

THE SKIN

A protective covering and a way to connect physically.

The health and well-being of the skin is vital. Just ask any teenager who suffers from acne about the impact poor skin has on their life. It is the largest organ of the body, which filters and releases toxins. It also protects, along with the bones and muscles, the vulnerable internal world of liquids and delicate organs. Without the skin, the body would have no separation or boundaries. The liquid mass of the body would be pouring out all over the place and just as your eyes can reflect how tired you are, the skin is one of the first wakeup calls that the internal world is failing.

If the skin is breaking out or drying up, this is a direct correlation to the whole system of the body being toxic or possibly dehydrated. It is actually better to be releasing waste through the skin rather than storing it in the body. Therefore, rashes, eczema, spots and flaking are all signs of the internal world desperately trying to release poisons.

Next time your skin reacts, pay attention. Are you taking a substance with which the body disagrees or is your detergent full of chemicals and causing irritation?

Look to the symptoms as a sign and then change the cause.

When you cover irritated skin with medicated creams, although it alleviates the symptoms, it also pushes the toxins back into the body exacerbating the long-term situation. This makes the body do the exact opposite of what its natural healing ability was attempting. Now the toxins are driven back into the body and a different elimination process has to begin.

Allow The Skin To Breathe

The skin, just like you, needs to breathe. If it is slathered continuously in clinical creams, make up, foundations and synthetic materials, the skin can suffocate. Think about what it feels like to throw open the windows on that first warm spring day and air out the house. The skin is no different. Each cell needs to be open and unclogged. This allows the skin to function at its optimum.

The Importance Of Sweating

Sweating is a good past time. Unfortunately you live in a world where sweating is not fashionable. Antiperspirants actually stop the flow of sweat. Sprays and perfumes cover up the smell. What is interesting is that if the body is in good health and clean internally, sweat has little or no odor. Take a moment to think back to the last time you worked up a good sweat. I hope that it was not that long ago. Lying on a beach or in a sauna does count. Any method, which allows the body to eliminate toxins through the pores, cleanses it. Obviously, it is vital to replenish the lost liquids by drinking plenty of pure water and adding some electrolytes, if needed.

The Skin And The Liver

The health of the skin has a direct correlation to the health of your liver. Those little brown or red spots on your skin are known as liver spots. It is a sign that the liver is congested or overwhelmed and is using the skin as a method to eliminate.

Care For The Skin

Female skin care products are a multi-billion dollar industry. Therefore, it is obvious that the appearance of the skin is of some importance. Interestingly, most of the pressure is to have clear wrinkle-free skin. Although this is a little 'ageist' the concept is to keep the skin healthy, vital and well nourished. This will result from your internal world being healthy. Not from the hundred-dollar face cream.

Unfortunately, much of what is promoted to beautify the skin is not actually beneficial for the rest of you. With this in mind, the quality of the products used on the skin is vital. One way to look at this is to ask the question whether you would be comfortable eating your moisturizers. What if you needed to give your organs a wash? Would you lather up your heart with some clinically toxic soap? Probably not. Well, the skin is also an organ and it absorbs whatever it meets.

Just as with food, read the ingredients of your skin care products. If you do not understand or cannot pronounce the words, put it back on the shelf and move on. Chemicals, laurel sulfates, alcohol, petroleum, mineral oil and colors are all readily absorbed into the blood stream. In the referral section of this guidebook, there are a number of high quality beauty lines, which distribute products with integrity and pure ingredients.

The Following are ways to keep your skin clean and healthy, breathing, and well fed:

Cleansing

This is an important part of your daily skin care routine.

The pores of the skin easily become clogged with dirt throughout the day and night. Therefore, it is essential to clean the skin, allowing it to breathe and receive the benefits of moisturizing.

- Choose a cleanser for your skin type.
- Avoid highly perfumed deodorants and soaps.
- Choose pure and natural ingredients in the products.
- Clean your face in the morning and in the evening.
- It is especially important to remove all make up or sunscreen at night so the skin can breathe and air out.

Exfoliation

Exfoliating allows the skin to breathe by sloughing off dead skin and encouraging new skin growth.

- **Exfoliating face scrubs.**
  These are good to use a few times a week. Pick one for your skin type and make sure whatever is being used does not scratch the skin.

- **Dry skin brushing.**
  This is an excellent way to clear dead skin, activate the lymph system and wake up the body.

- ◆ **Salt or sugar scrubs.**
  These can be used on the whole body. They often contain oils, therefore leaving the skin moisturized.

- ◆ **Loofas and Sponges.**
  They can be used with natural soaps. Keep them clean and replace often.

Masks

Masks are a wonderful way to nourish, cleanse and rejuvenate the skin.

Masks also encourage you to have a sense of humor about yourself as your face is covered with an attractive shade of green stuff! Another benefit is that they tend to slow you down and make you move less, as it is limiting as to what you will try to accomplish slathered up with suds. You can also be quite inventive and frugal when it comes to making your own facemasks. Some left over avocado or strawberries and cream can make excellent homemade remedies.

Toning and serums

Using natural toning solutions and serums help balance the skin's pH.
Depending on the ingredients, these solutions can feed the skin and prepare the face and neck for a moisturizer. Pay attention that the toner does not dry out your skin.

Moisturizing

Feeding, nourishing and replenishing the skin.

Whenever moisturizer is applied onto the body, it is readily absorbed into the tissue and blood stream. Therefore, thoroughly check the quality and choose only pure and natural ingredients. It depends on the climate as to how much moisturizer the body needs. The hotter and sunnier the weather, the drier the body gets, therefore the more moisturizer it requires. The skin on the face, neck, chest and hands is very delicate and calls for more moisturizing. There are actually no oil pores in the skin around the eyes. Hence, it is one of the first places to wrinkle. Thus, this is an area to moisturize at least twice a day. The hands also tend to get dry because they are being washed more often than other body parts; consequently, it is a good idea to carry some hand cream around with you.

Deodorant

A little bit of sweat is a natural occurrence

The underarm is a natural place for the body to perspire and release toxins. Therefore, when the pores are blocked the toxins have to be stored. The beauty is, the cleaner your diet, the less you smell.

- **Antiperspirants stop the flow of sweat from under the arms, which can be detrimental to breast health.**
  Toxins tend to get stored in fat cells if they cannot be released and the breasts are full of fatty tissue.

- **Aluminum is a product often used in deodorants.**
  Because of the possible risk factors, aluminum-free products are recommended.

- **Choose a natural deodorant.**
  There are many great choices nowadays, just read the ingredients.

Sun Block And Sunshine

It is all about balance. The body needs sunshine to absorb vitamin D, yet too much can cause skin damage and a dry, wrinkled texture.

- **Twenty minutes of direct sunshine is recommended each day.**
  For most Californians, this is easy enough. For the English, good luck with this.

- **The skin does need to be protected from the UV rays of the sun.**
  However, do pay attention to the ingredients in the sunscreen.

- **Titanium dioxide is a healthier possibility, rather than the use of chemicals.**

- **Covering up the body with hats and shirts obviously protects against too much harmful exposure.**

- **Wash off the sunscreen once out of the sun and to reapply as needed.**

- **Eminence Body Care and DHC Products both carry excellent sun blocks.**

*"What spirit is so empty and blind,
that it cannot recognize the fact that the foot is more noble
than the shoe and skin more beautiful
than the garment with which it is clothed?"
~Michelangelo*

Supplementing The Skin

The skin needs food just like the body.

The major ingredients are:

◆ **Water to rehydrate.**

◆ **Essential fatty acids.**
Found in fish oils, evening primrose oil, coconut oil, olive oil, flax oil and some foods such as avocados and walnuts. These are to be taken internally.

◆ **Certain nutrients and minerals.**
Such as vitamin C, zinc, vitamins A and E.

◆ **High quality moisturizers and oils to be used topically.**

The Effects Of Water On The Body

The majority of the body is made up of water.

◆ **By drinking plenty of pure water, the physicality of the body is replenished.**

◆ **Soaking and bathing in water helps you to relax.**

◆ **Water tends to have a soothing effect on the nervous system.**

◆ **Water keeps the body clean.**

◆ **Soft water tends to be less drying on the skin than hard water.**
The hardness of the water depends on where you live.

◆ **Hot water or steam opens up the pores releasing toxins.**
By ending with a cold shower or splashing the face with cold water, helps the pores close back up.

◆ **The Kangen Beauty Water (Ph 5.5) literally has a beautifying effect on the skin.**

Kangen Beauty Water

This is actually called beauty water because it is the exact PH of the skin, which is 5.5. It is used as a spray or to wash with or to rinse the hair and body at the end of a bath or shower. The results are softer, subtler, more youthful skin. This water is collected from the Kangen Water machine; additionally, there is a Kangen Shower filter available.

Baths

Bathing in a body of water has to be one of the most relaxing and pampering pastimes.

The following are options to enhance the detoxifying qualities of a bath time:

- **Add one pound of Epson salt to the bath and soak for twenty minutes.**

- **Add one pound of Epson bath salt and one pound of baking soda to the bath and soak for twenty minutes.**
  Both methods will detoxify the body, clear the energy field and is especially beneficial for tired and sore muscles. Rinse thoroughly afterwards and drink an extra glass of water to replenish.

- **Add aromatherapy oils to enhance the mood of the bath.**
  - Lavender and Chamomile will aid relaxation.
  - Rosemary and Peppermint help clear the mind.
  - Tea tree, Sandalwood and Ylang-ylang help bladder or yeast infections.
  - Eucalyptus to aid with respiratory ailments.

- **Add almond oil to the bath.**
  Adding almond oil to the bath acts as a carrier for the essential oils giving your skin a long lasting smooth and healthy texture.

MAKEUP

Adorning the image you present to the world.

Make up is another interesting dilemma. It can make you feel beautiful, feminine and enhance all the right features, yet if what is being placed on the skin is toxic, full of chemicals and does not let the skin breathe, there is an obvious problem. Whatever is placed on the skin is absorbed into the body. It is recommended to choose products with natural and beneficial ingredients and then adorn yourself with a clean conscience.

- **Always remove make up at night.**
  Choose a makeup remover that is natural and non-toxic. You can use one of the companies in the Referral Section.

- **Change your mascara every three months.**
  It can easily accumulate bacteria.

- **Keep your make up tools clean.**
  This includes sponges and brushes.

- **Do not share makeup.**

- **Pay attention to the ingredients in lipstick, lip-gloss and Chap Stick.**
  You will ingest these substances when you eat.

- **For periods of time go naked.**
  This means go without make up or nail polish and allow your skin and nails to breathe, receive sunlight, vitamins and more readily absorb moisture.

INTERNAL CLEANSING

Your external appearance is a direct correlation to the health of your internal body.

The condition of your skin, hair, and nails and the clarity of your eyes are all telltale signs as to what is happening on the inside of your body.

Just as you clean your hair, car or closet, your organs also need the odd bath. There are many choices, some sweeter, others more intense. Therefore, depending on the severity of your symptoms, which can range from skin disorders to an actual disease, choose what is appropriate for you. It is always better to start with baby steps and graduate to the more advanced methods.

Yet the first and most important step is to eliminate constipation.

It is actually detrimental to try to cleanse the body if it does not have an evacuation outlet. Bowel movements are the safest and the most effective way to eliminate toxins and old residue. If this avenue is not open, whatever is being released has to find a new home in the body, which could be even more harmful.

Remember the human body has its own intelligence.

If a poisonous substance is ingested the body has three choices:

- **First, it can quickly eliminate the toxin through vomiting or diarrhea.**

- **Second, it can transform the problem into a less harmful substance.**
  This allows it to pass through the body and eventually be released through the urine, a bowel movement, mucus or even the skin. This type of cleansing could also come in the form of a rash.

- **Third, if the above methods are not viable, the body will store the poison.**
  This can be because the body is dehydrated or not enough fiber is being ingested, causing constipation, which blocks the body's ability to cleanse. The toxins then accumulate in the liver or fatty tissue. As you probably realize, these poisons remain in the body. Eventually they will need to be released or disease can occur.

By finding methods to internally cleanse the body, you will keep yourself healthy and in balance. Cleansing is not just to be done once a year, but on a daily basis. This can be as simple as eating some ground flax seed or a glass of fresh lemon juice and water.

Ways To Keep The Internal Body Clean:

Remedies help to keep the body toxin-free.

- **Drink plenty of clean, pure water.**
  This literally will flush out debris.

- **Exercise.**
  This helps the body sweat and eliminate. A small trampoline such as a rebounder is particularly beneficial as it stimulates the lymph system, which is the body's natural housekeeper.

- **Add probiotics.**
  Friendly bacteria will balance the digestive tract and help with elimination.

- **Use a dry skin brush.**
  This encourages the skin to detoxify and sloughs off dead skin cells.

- **Drink hot water and fresh lemon juice upon waking.**
  This helps the liver cleanse and encourages elimination.

- **Add raw, unfiltered apple cider vinegar into your diet.**
  This helps bring the body back to a more alkaline condition.

◆ **Make up a batch of Bieler's Broth and drink 2-3 cups a day.**
This aids in cleansing the liver. You can find this recipe by searching "Bieler's Broth" online.

◆ **Increase the amount of high quality fiber you ingest.**
An example is ground flax seed, which can be used on a daily basis. Fiber is like sweeping out the house. The dust and dirt is collected as it travels through the system and then released. Make sure you are drinking plenty of water with the fiber.

◆ **Increase certain foods to aid in cleansing the body.**
Examples are fresh beets. They go in red and come out red, just so you know! Asparagus, shitake mushrooms, daikon radish, and cultured vegetables are other good examples. Look for delicious recipes in *'The Versatile Vegetable'* cookbook.

◆ **Stop eating between 6 or 7 in the evening.**
This allows the liver to cleanse the body and the digestive system to fast and rest until morning.

◆ **Drinking Kangan™ water naturally detoxifies the body.**
If you are taking medications, it is important that you drink only clean water in the beginning.

◆ **Enemas and colonics are effective ways to relieve constipation.**
This detoxifies the body. Make sure you choose a recommended, educated and knowledgeable colon therapist.

◆ **Massage, including lymph drainage, is highly beneficial.**
Yet, any body massage will aid the body's ability to detoxify itself.

◆ **Herbal Cleanses.**
There are many choices out there. It is recommended that you be under the supervision of a trained practitioner for direction and guidance.

- **Juice Fasting.**
  Drinking only liquids for a day gives the digestive system a rest and allows the body to clean house. Make sure to keep your blood sugar levels balanced by drinking every couple of hours. Possible liquids include water, vegetable juices, blended soups or broths, Bieler's Broth, smoothies, warm water and fresh lemon juice, water and apple cider vinegar, powdered green super foods with water, Bio K and probiotic drinks. When cleansing, do not overlook any symptoms you might be experiencing. Headaches, rashes, irritability and fatigue are all excellent signs of a body cleanse and need to be honored. Make time for Epson salt baths, naps, exercise, Yoga Nidra and movement. These rituals allow the body to repair and heal. There is no point in giving the body the tools to detoxify if all your energy is being used for other activities. In fact, this can be harmful. Any detoxification program asks the organs of elimination, such as the liver, kidneys and colon, to work extra hard to cleanse the body. They need energy to do this.

Cleansing the internal body takes energy. Therefore, honor the time and resources spent by not reloading the system with unhealthy choices.

HONORING MENSTRUATION
The womb is the seat of the sacred feminine.

Bleeding or the moon cycle as it can be called, is a natural feminine rhythm. It allows the body to detoxify itself after the possibility of pregnancy has passed. In some traditions, the time of a woman's menses is honored as sacred and she is allowed to rest, be by herself or with other women and is relieved of her daily duties. Just imagine! Instead, here in the West where it is business as usual, women are taught to bulldoze through whatever 'To Do' list is in front of them, ignore the impatience and irritability they feel, and then you wonder why people give you terrifying looks.

Pre-Menstrual Syndrome has a whole story of its own. As a woman, you know the impact that hormones can have. The cleaner the body and the more exquisite the self-care is, the sweeter the period. Some of the benefits include less or no cramping, a gentler flow, a decrease in mood swings and irritability, no headaches and a lighter, regular period. The latter is vital if you are trying to get pregnant.

Yet there is another side to this ebb and flow of your cycle, which is often ignored.

What if the build up to the period was a true read of how your life was actually going? With the onslaught of hormones, you can no longer temper your mood, emotions or reactions. How this translates is if you have a week from hell before your bleeding, you may want to pay attention to this emotional roller coaster and notice if you are authentically living your life. A lack of creativity, play and sensuality can be a major player in the battle with PMS. Instead of blaming the unleashed she devil, honor the raw intensity of your inner emotional being and listen to what she is screaming at you.

Be authentic to yourself.

Imagine a month when your period came and took you by surprise because there were so few symptoms leading up to it! Imagine napping when you felt like it, curling up with a good book and a hot water bottle, taking a bath or simply not having to talk to anyone.

Now instead of just dreaming, turn this into a reality. Yes, life goes on, but next month it can be tempered by slowing down the pace and taking more loving care of you.

> *"In man, the shedding of blood is always associated with injury, disease, or death. Only the female half of humanity was seen to have the magical ability to bleed profusely and still rise phoenix-like each month from the gore."*
> ~ Estelle R. Ramey

◆ Sugar Cravings

The body naturally craves sweet foods before your period. This is because sugar causes a sense of expansion in the body and therefore allows the blood to flow more easily. Obviously, this sugar craving can cause mischief if unhealthy choices are made. Therefore, instead of a candy bar, go for a piece of fresh fruit and reduce your salt intake.

◆ Chocolate Cravings

When you crave chocolate around your period, it is often the body's need for magnesium. Instead of eating a chocolate bar, try taking a magnesium supplement. The powdered magnesium supplement 'Calm', by Natural Vitality is highly recommended. It helps with elimination, calms the nerves and allows you to sleep better too.

"Interestingly when I take magnesium throughout the month, I can easily walk away from chocolate. Yet if I haven't and it is around my cycle, I would possibly fight for the last piece." ~ Miranda

Ways To Conquer The Rage Monster

- **Exercise can be highly beneficial in helping to eliminate painful periods.**
  Begin with some kind of gentle movement such as walking, swimming or yoga.

- **Choose sanitary products that are made from natural ingredients.**
  This means they are free from perfumes, chlorine bleach, petro chemicals and deodorants. If you can buy organic cotton pads or tampons, that is even better!

- **Try using pads rather than tampons whenever possible.**
  This allows a natural flow of blood, easing cramping. Think of a cork in a bottle!

- **Cuddle up with a hot water bottle to ease stomach cramps.**

- **Drink a cup of warm, calming tea, such as chamomile, peppermint or ginger.**

- **Acupuncture or non-force chiropractic adjustments can be highly beneficial for any ongoing problems with your period or infertility.**

- **Take a nap or some quiet time to honor the natural inclination to be still.**

- **Let people know, and educate them on how you are feeling ahead of time, therefore, they know not to demand too much from you.**

Menopause

*One of life's natural transitions
and a time to go inward and inquire into the self.*

Just as your periods need to be honored, so do the precious transitions into menopause do. This is a transformational period for women (no pun intended) as the drive and instinct to reproduce is replaced by an internal journey. If this time is honored and allowed, it can lead to great inner wisdom and the grace that comes with age.

If you choose to take exquisite care of the body, deeply listen, support and acknowledge its messages through this process of change, the outcome will be a temple, which will house you for many more years to come.

There is a tendency during this time for the body to lose its moisture and suppleness. Therefore, be conscious to replenish with plenty of water, healthy fats and oils, live foods rich in vitamins and minerals to stay vitalized, juicy and healthy.

Many of the remedies for menstruation can also be helpful during menopause. The better care you take of your body in your earlier years will often translate into an easier transition during menopause.

- **During menopause, honor the body's messages to slow down, rejuvenate and travel inward.**

- **Keep the body hydrated.**

- **Moisturize the skin and hair thoroughly.**

- **Increase the amount of essential fatty acids, such as fish and vegetable oils and evening primrose oil.**

- **Diet can play a major role in calming and supporting you through this transition.**

- There are certain foods to increase and others to avoid.
  Eat sea vegetables, gelatin, healthy fats and mineral rich foods. Limit hot spicy foods, alcohol, refined flour and sugar, table salt and unhealthy fats.

- If you experience hot flashes, avoid caffeine, spices, sugar and alcohol.

- Get your hormone levels checked, if your symptoms are problematic.

- There are many natural ways to replace hormones, if this speaks to you.

- Healing modalities such as Acupuncture, Chinese Herbs or Homeopathy can be highly beneficial in elevating symptoms and helping the body to adjust.

- Breath work can help with cooling the body.
  During inhalation, curl up both edges of the tongue so that it forms of tube. As you curl your tongue, slightly protrude it through the lips while slowly breathing in through the mouth. (It seems 1 in 3 people are unable to curl their tongue, so if you are one of the special ones, just lay your tongue on the lower teeth.) Close the mouth and breathe out through your nose. This is called the 'air conditioning breath' and the moisture in the mouth cools the air as it enters the body. Repeat 6-10 times while you are experiencing a hot flash.

The healthier the body, the easier the transition.

BREAST AND FEMININE CARE

Breasts are the symbol of womanhood and the ability to nourish and nurture the self and others.

Just ask any man, breasts and cleavage are one of the wonders of the world! They have the ability to nourish another human being. When someone is hurting, you hold them to your breast to bring comfort. Breasts are ultimately feminine and are not to be ignored.

- **Choose bras made of natural, breathable fibers, such as cotton.**
  This allows the skin and tissue of the breast to breath.

- **Eliminate underwire bras as much as possible.**
  Save them for that special occasion.

- **Make sure the bra fits well and supports you.**
  The tissue of the breast is delicate and it is not good for it to be compressed on a daily basis.

- **Get a yearly breast exam with your gynecologist.**
  Include a pap smear with the check up.

- **Check your own breasts on a weekly basis.**
  Allow yourself to get to know this area of the body well. You should take notice how they feel. The tissue of the breast often changes with the menstrual cycle and the intake of caffeine or chocolate. Become familiar with your breasts' natural terrain so you have a reference for comparison during your cycle.

◆ **Massage your own breasts, underarms and surrounding area.**
Use your own loving touch to honor and adore this completely feminine terrain. This is where many toxins are stored and lymph nodes live. Therefore, by massaging the area you will be releasing any build up, keeping your breasts and underarms healthy, and receiving attention. A wonderful way to honor and love your breasts is to massage them gently in a circular motion on a daily basis. This works well while you are in the shower or moisturizing your body. They say if you want larger breasts the circles will start in the center of the chest moving up and towards the outside of your body. If you would like smaller breasts massage in the opposite direction.

◆ **Choose a natural, non-toxic, nonaluminum deodorant.**
This will allow the body to eliminate poisons naturally. Sweating is a natural process and removes toxins from the fatty tissues of the breasts.

The breasts are an exquisite symbol of your femininity.
Therefore, treat them lovingly.

THE HAIR

Symbolizes strength and your self-image relationship.

How annoying is it that a good hair day is a better day and that a bad hair day or haircut for that matter, can ruin many a good moment. Why is it that hair is so important? Well it frames your face, either complimenting your features or not. Billions of dollars are spent promoting the perfect shampoo, color or conditioner. Therefore, it seems as though there is a strong comparison with the state of your hair and your self-worth. Whether this is a good or not is debatable, but on a more basic level, the strength, condition and shine of your hair is a direct result to your internal health. If your hair is dry and brittle so are you. You might need more water, oils, or both.

"When I was young I dreaded getting my hair cut. To save money the hairdresser was told to keep my bangs short. In my opinion I was left with way too much forehead showing and I distinctly remember it affecting my self-confidence and spending hours pulling on my bangs to try and make them longer." ~ Miranda

Hair Care Tips

The products that you put on your head have an effect on your hair and overall well-being. Alcohol can be treacherous and many hair care products do have it tucked away in their list of ingredients, even the so-called healthy ones.

- **Limit heat on the hair.**
  Heat is extremely damaging to hair. You do have the opportunity to save the environment and your hair by avoiding the use of such appliances. It seems as though the better the haircut, the less attention and grooming it needs.

- **Brush the hair.**
  This distributes the natural oils to the ends of your hair, making it shiny and healthy-looking. It also feels good. At the very least, you might consider doing this before you wash your hair.

- ◆ **Oil your hair.**
  This is a great way to condition your hair and if you choose, you can leave it on overnight, therefore thoroughly penetrating your scalp and hair. Try jojoba, coconut or olive oil or conditioners. Please check for healthy ingredients, however.

- ◆ **Alcohol, laurel sulphate and any other ingredient that you cannot pronounce or do not have a clue as to what it is, are to be avoided.**
  They are literally soaking into your brain.

- ◆ **Apple cider vinegar can be a good rinse for your hair and often cuts through any residue left from shampoos and conditioners.**
  Approximately one-quarter cup to one cup of water is adequate.

- ◆ **Use natural hair coloring.**
  It is less damaging to your hair. Look for ones that are peroxide free.

"The beauty of a woman is not in the clothes she wears, the figure that she carries or the way she combs her hair."
~ Audrey Hepburn

HAIR REMOVAL
Becoming truly naked.

Removing unwanted body hair seems to be a very feminine pastime and there are many options. While you may be removing the hair for esthetic and beauty's sake, you need to be careful as you may also be damaging the skin.

The Following Are Methods Of Hair Removal:
Some are certainly easier on the body than others are.

- **Shaving.**
  This old-fashioned method does the trick without too much damage to the skin, as long as you are careful to avoid cutting yourself! Always make sure the razor is clean, relatively new, belongs to you and sharp. Never leave a razor face down as it will rust. If you suffer from ingrown hairs, as you might know, shaving can be a problem. Always shave in the direction of the hair growth.

- **Plucking.**
  Obviously good for small areas, it is free and does the trick, yet obviously very time consuming for larger areas.

- **Waxing.**
  Painful, yet effective and apart from the trauma of ripping cooled wax off the skin layer, it is relatively harmless and lasts longer than shaving. Ingrown hairs can be a problem if you are prone to them.

- **Depilatory Cream.**
  Pay attention to these creams because if they are strong enough to dissolve a hair, the ingredients are certainly strong enough to damage the skin surface and more importantly, it will be absorbed into the blood stream.

- **Electrolysis.**
  This is an old, tried and tested method of hair removal. The good news is that particular hair will never grow back. The bad news is that each hair follicle has up to three growth cycles; therefore, it can often take a while to become a hairless wonder. The other downside is that it is expensive, repetitive and painful. Yet for small problem areas, it can be highly effective.

- **Laser.**
  This method of hair removal is relatively new. The upside is that it removes large areas of hair at once. The downside is the expense and the damage it can cause to the skin layer and possibly the body.

THE EYES

The doorway to the soul and the ability to see and perceive.

Much can be revealed through the eyes. When someone is lying, unless they are pathological liars, they tend not to make eye contact, hence the expression 'look me in the eye'. In addition, if you are truly exhausted your eyes cannot pretend. Unfortunately, these extraordinary sensory organs are taking a beating these days.

Think about how many times you use your eyes to work on a computer or to watch a screen. Have you noticed how your eyes feel after a few hours? Small screens have become such a part of daily life nowadays that it is vital to remember to pull your vision away from the single point and to relax the eyes from working so hard.

Be aware of how many hours you and your loved ones are spending in front of electronics. Give your eyes a break. Switch your focus from detailed work to gross motor activities such as walking, running or swimming.

There are a number of eye exercises to relieve eyestrain and it is highly recommended that they become part of your regular daily routine, along with kegals.

Eye Exercises And Treatments:
Curiously, when you take the time to exercise one part of the body, the rest will tend to respond and relax as well.

◆ **Move away from the screen and allow your eyes to be exercised and stretched by reversing their focus from a single point to the periphery.**
Start by looking up as far as your eyes will go. Then look down. Now look right and then left. Stretch your eyes by looking from one diagonal point to the next. First look to the above right corner and then to the lower left corner. Now look to the above left corner and then to the lower right corner. Take notice how your eyes feel. Avoid straining and continue to find these points on the periphery with your eyes until they feel relaxed and revitalized.

◆ **Relax your eyes by rotating them in along the periphery of your vision.**
Move slowly and gently in a clockwise and then counter clockwise direction.

◆ **Hold your finger approximately three inches from your nose.**
Look at your finger and then look away at something in the distance. Continue this near and far gaze. You are asking your eyes to refocus from one object to another. Keep your head still as your eyes move.

◆ **Place your feet about hip width apart.**
Begin to twist at the waist while keeping your feet planted firmly on the ground. Twist slowly and comfortably while swinging your arms from side to side. If you feel dizzy, you are moving too fast. Now consciously choose a point to focus on with your eyes as you twist your trunk. For example, choose a point behind you and each time you twist around, focus your eyes on that same point.

◆ **Sit and vigorously rub your hands together creating warmth between them. Then cup your hands over your closed eyes and relax.**
Take a few deep breaths while you are here. If you practice Reiki, you can give your eyes a brief Reiki treatment.

◆ **Cucumber slices or damp chamomile tea bags provide relief to tired or strained eyes.**
Simply place them on your closed eyelids as you lie down to rest. Deep breathing will always enhance your relaxation.

◆ **A beauty note: There are no natural oil glands around the area of the eyes.**
Moisturize the delicate skin surrounding the eyes in the morning and evening, keeping these precious doorways to the soul vital and healthy looking.

"The health of the eye seems to demand a horizon.
We are never tired, so long as we can see far enough."
~ Emerson

THE EARS
The ability to truly listen and discern.

If you have ever had an earache or vertigo you will know the importance of keeping this sense organ healthy. The ears affect both your balance and hearing. In Chinese medicine, it is said that the ears in the shape of an embryo represent the whole body. The head being the lobe, the outside ridge being the spine, the organs and limbs all curled up on the inside, just like a baby in a womb. So to massage the ears can be pleasurable and healing. Because of their size, you can do a full body massage in a few minutes. Pay attention to any areas that are tender and massage a little longer.

Cleaning The Ears:
The inner and middle ear are extremely delicate areas of the body.

- **When using cotton swabs to clean the ears, you must not to probe too deep.**
  The body has its own ability to cleanse itself, by bringing excess wax to the surface. By digging around, you can cause significant damage.

- **If you have an earache, warmed olive oil and garlic can be a good remedy or you can buy natural eardrops.**

- **Hydrogen peroxide will fizz and bubble but is also highly effective.**

- **Ear Coning.**
  This ancient system of cleaning the ears is also known as ear coning or candling. Long thin cones made of linen and wax are used by inserting the narrow end of the cone into the ear then lighting the wide end on fire. The heat draws out excess wax from the ear canal. It is a gentle and effective way of removing a build-up of wax because the heat softens the wax and allows it to be drawn out by suction. This method can be used as maintenance about every four to six months and more often if you feel your sinuses are blocked or you have a cold or an earache. It can also help ringing in the ears and issues with balance. This is not a practice to do to yourself. The ears are a delicate part of your body and need to be treated with respect, so find a trained practitioner.

THE NOSE
where the breath of life enters and the ability to discern.

The nose is another vital body part. By using the sense of smell, you know straight away whether you like it or not. A certain smell can flood you with memories, good or bad. A foul smell will repel you as far away as possible, a clear sign not to eat or touch it. Yet, an appealing smell will draw all your senses in towards the object. Think of smelling a beautiful garden rose or food that is highly appealing to you. The expression 'It smells good enough to eat' sums it up.

The nose is also the main channel for the breath. It actually filters much more efficiently than the mouth, as it has hairs to trap germs and dust. Infections can often begin in the nose or sinus cavities; hence, it is an important area to keep clear. The reason the body produces mucus when you have a cold is to help eliminate the virus or bacteria. Every time you sneeze or blow your nose, some of the virus or bacteria leave the infected area. Therefore, blow your nose rather than sniffling and whenever possible, allow the body to drain itself, rather than taking medications, which dry up the symptoms and do not allow the body to heal itself.

These are natural home remedies to use in caring for the nasal passages:

- **Netti Pot.**
  The nose has its own filter system of thousands of tiny hairs. Yet, certain dust and bacteria still get through. If you have ever suffered from a sinus infection, you know how blocked and uncomfortable it is when this system cannot do its job effectively. One way to keep the nostrils clear and open is to use an old Indian system called a Netti pot. It looks like an Aladdin's lamp. At first, it may seem a little awkward, but as with anything, practice makes perfect, especially if you use the Netti pot daily. Follow the procedure on the box or the directions below:

Fill the pot with filtered warm water and high-quality fine-ground sea salt. Make sure it is not too hot. Turn your head to the side and slightly drop the forehead down so the water travels through the nose and not down the throat. Place the tip of the pot in one nostril, allowing the warm saline solution to pour through that nostril and out the other, flushing out any debris. By repeating on the other side, both nostrils are cleansed. You will notice a refreshing ability to breathe clearly again. It also aids in preventing head colds by keeping the sinuses and nasal passages clear.

"I use the Netti Pot daily in the shower and swear that it is what keeps me from catching many of the bugs floating around." ~ *Miranda*

- **Steam.**
  By standing in a hot shower or placing your head above a bowl of steaming water, you can loosen congestion and alleviate symptoms caused by a head cold. Aromatherapy oils, such as eucalyptus, can also be added.

- **Saline or Xylitol nasal spray.**
  Both of these spray solutions work well to keep the nose clear.

- **Acupuncture, Chiropractic, Massage or Acupressure.**
  These healing modalities can help alleviate symptoms, especially if you get sinus headaches.

THE TEETH

A smile, a greeting, a way of breaking life down into acceptable pieces and the ability to defend yourself.

Similar to many of the other holistic, self-care movements today, the care of your teeth is an area where self-education and awareness will serve you well.

It is fascinating to look back in history to the life of a toothbrush. Once it was only for the rich, everyone else got to use their fingers or a rag. Yet now due to modern miracles toothbrushes are affordable and easy to buy. This simple practice of cleaning your teeth twice daily, along with flossing, is what will keep your teeth and gums strong, healthy and in your mouth. Much research has been done in conjunction with gum disease and your overall health. It has been shown that by daily flossing you can add ten years to your life. This is because the low-grade infections found in the mouth slowly but surely chip away at the immune system. Regular daily flossing takes care of this.

There are holistic minded dentists. Specifically, these doctors are abreast of the techniques and methods to care for your mouth and teeth without incurring damage or side effects to the rest of the body. Mercury laced fillings are an example of dental practices of the past, that while they remedied the hole in the tooth, the body suffered an infusion of toxic heavy metal into its system. If you have mercury fillings, you may want to look into their removal. Make sure to find a dentist who follows the proper procedures such as cupping the throat so the body does not absorb the mercury. In addition, they will be able to recommend remedies to help your body rid itself of the toxins. This procedure will relieve burdens on both your nervous and immune systems.

Anytime your teeth become cracked, diseased or abscessed, your blood, digestion, immune system and spinal alignment may be affected. If you are in the practice of visiting a chiropractor regularly, inform them about any recent dental treatments so that your whole system may be checked out. On your own, maintain an awareness of your general health one to two weeks after any dental surgery or repairing procedure. Be sensitive to swelling, soreness, headaches or general malaise. To take care of your teeth and gums directly correlates to the health of your whole body. It is often a good idea to give the body extra nutrients to help it absorb toxins after dental work. Examples of this are fish oils, turmeric for inflammation, cilantro, chlorophyll or parsley to mop up any heavy metals and plenty of pure water to help flush the system. It is interesting to note that once an infection or problem in the mouth is healed, other areas of the body feel better too. This correlates to each tooth being connected directly to specific parts of the body and organs. Once the tooth is better so is its connected organ or vise versa.

Regular Home Dental Care Includes:

- Brush your teeth twice a day.

- Change your toothbrushes every three months.

- Use an electric toothbrush.

- Have regular check-ups with your dentist.

- Floss daily.

- Use a tongue cleaner twice a day.

- Choose an alcohol-free mouthwash.

- Choose fluoride-free toothpaste.

- Use a gum massager.

◆ Choose gum sweetened with Xylitol, a natural, antibacterial agent that may inhibit cavities. It can also be used when brushing is not convenient.

◆ Home remedies, such as brushing with baking soda and using hydrogen peroxide as a mouthwash, have also proved useful, safe and effective.

"Growing up my dentist was called 'Dr. Puller' and even though he had pictures of little kittens on the ceiling he terrified me. Hence when he told me that brushing my teeth twice a day would mean not needing to visit the dentist as much, I was convinced." ~ Miranda

THE JAW

*By softening and relaxing the jaw,
emotions such as anger and resentment can be released.*

The jaw is an area of the body that is highly useful when it comes to chewing, but if the joint is tight or tense, it can cause a medley of problems such as headaches, neck pain or TMJ, as it is commonly known. TMJ occurs when the jaw joint is locked or tightened. Massaging the area can help. Notice if you are grinding or clenching your teeth, this can happen while you are sleeping too. If so, a visit to a dentist for a mouth guard may be in order. Many emotions are held in the jaw, especially anger. Look at what truth may need to be spoken.

Ways To Take Care Of The Jaw:

- **Ultimately, releasing and relaxing the jaw is all about consciousness.**
  Next time you try to open a jar that is too tight, notice how actively involved your jaw becomes. Did your teeth clench and grind together or did you use the strength in your arms or hands instead? Try relaxing the jaw, activating the kegals and using your arm strength.

- **When you are feeling stressed, notice if you have a space between the teeth.**
  If not, open the mouths slightly, wiggle the jaw back and forth keeping space there as you go about your day.

- **Practice softening your tongue.**
  Surprisingly, the tongue is the strongest muscle in the body and this simple action relaxes the whole area of the jaw.

- ◆ **Cranial sacral or non-force chiropractic work.**
  Both of these healing modalities can help alleviate symptoms.

- ◆ **Laughing and smiling are brilliant activities for your health and well-being.**
  It takes more facial muscles to frown, than it does to smile and releases endorphins. This is much easier than exercising!

"Better slip with foot than tongue."
~ Benjamin Franklin

THE TONGUE

*The ability to communicate
and taste the pleasures or bitterness of life.*

The tongue is actually the strongest muscle in the body. In Chinese medicine, it is used as a diagnostic tool. If your tongue is swollen, coated in a white layer, has spots or is cracked, this is a sign of an imbalance somewhere else in the body. Keeping the tongue clean is of utmost importance, just like the teeth.

This means the tongue can be used as a daily gage and diagnostic tool for your overall health. Ideally, it is pinkish, clear and sweet tasting. All of your taste buds are on the tongue, therefore if it is coated this limits the ability to fully enjoy flavors. This could be seen as a crime where certain foods are concerned.

Cleaning The Tongue:
The tongue can be cleansed with your toothbrush, but much more effectively, with a tongue cleaner. These little scraping devices help to clean the surface of the tongue, which sweetens the breath and removes waste from the mouth. They are simple to use and are sold in health food stores. Use one every time you brush.

THE THROAT AND NECK

The bottleneck, which balances the spiritual plane with the physical.

The throat is the seat of communication and is also a natural bottleneck in the body; hence it can easily get sore and infected. By speaking your truth, you will help the area energetically stay healthy and clear.

◆ If you get a sore throat, gargle with hot water and sea salt immediately.

◆ Eliminate any sugars as this feeds the infection.

◆ Hot water, honey, lemon juice and fresh ginger will soothe the throat.

◆ Wearing blue or turquoise around the neck invokes healing energy.

◆ Supporting the neck and head while sleeping is vital.

◆ Foam pillows can be more effective than down because they help to support the cervical curve of the neck while sleeping.

THE HANDS

Expression, creativity and how to handle life's situations.

Hands along with feet are treated rather like the poor cousin. They work hard; achieving great ends, yet receive very little acclaim or gratitude. You use your hands continuously. Even when you are talking, you express through them. Much of artistic creation is achieved through the hands. They accomplish task after task from sending emails to washing up. They can caress yet punch when needed. They can beckon or reject and they certainly can be a living expression of who you are.

Ways To Take Care Of Your Hands:

- **Keep your hands moisturized.**
  The hands can get dry because they, along with the chest, are exposed to the most sun. In addition, washing them or doing dishes can dry them out. Therefore, moisturize them regularly and carry a small, natural hand moisturizer in your bag.

- **Stretch your hands.**
  If you have been writing on the computer, take a moment to stretch out the fingers as far as possible. Just like the rest of the body, they do not want to stay in the same position for too long. You can also buy stress balls that you squeeze and let go of, to stimulate and strengthen the hand muscles.

- **Wear gloves any time you are dealing with toxic substances.**
  Whatever the skin touches is then absorbed into the body.

- **Keep the nails and cuticles clean and groomed.**
  This symbolizes love and care of the self.

- **Use your hands to create.**
  Life is not all about work and chores. Use these amazing instruments to express your creativity, whatever your calling.

◆ **Massage your hands.**
Hand massages can be relaxing and helpful to release stress and tension.

◆ **Remember the power of touch.**
For yourself and your loved ones.

THE FEET
Being grounded and finding your direction in life.

The feet are often ignored, left to their own devices, out on a limb literally. Yet in reality, they are vital. They bear the weight of your whole body, with many intricate bones knitted together for support. They ground you to the earth plain and without your toes you would find it very difficult to balance.

Therefore, next time you are in a bath or a forward bend, check to see how your feet are doing. Often they are stuffed into shoes too tight, stood on all day, and treated like workhorses. Spend some time pampering, moisturizing, removing calluses or soaking them. They are what take you in the direction you need to go in life. It seems as though they deserve some attention and respect.

"I have often wondered about high pointy heels and tight skirts. It seems as though both adornments result in a woman being ungrounded and unable to run or defend herself leaving her rather powerless. It is interesting as how what we deem as beautiful can also be so disempowering." ~ Miranda

Ways To Care For Your Feet:

◆ **Stretch your feet and toes.**
Yoga is wonderful for the feet. You can also spend some time curling your toes, spreading them or standing on your tiptoes.

◆ **Check for fungus and athletes foot.**
This area is ripe for fungus and mold. It can be a sign that you may have internal issues with Candida, yeasts and mold. Probiotics are a great internal remedy for this. Tea tree oil is a wonderful external preventative and cure if caught early. Douse the area with the oil daily.

◆ **Keep your nails clean and cut correctly.**
This will stop ingrown toenails from forming.

- ◈ **Remove nail polish regularly.**
  This allows the nails to go without polish for periods of time. Also, let them get some sun with no polish on them. This will keep the nails from turning brown because they are able to breathe. Remember most nail polish and removers are highly toxic.

- ◈ **Check your shoes fit well.**
  Find shoes that support your feet. This is especially important for walking, running and hiking shoes. Ideally, you should be able to bend the shoe, which means it has the flexibility your feet naturally need. Beauty is not worth the damage caused by wearing shoes that are too tight, too high or unsupportive on a regular basis.

- ◈ **Go Barefoot as much as possible.**
  Do what nature intended from time to time.

- ◈ **Check for bunions and calluses.**
  These are signs of the feet not getting the support they need. 'Pedeggs' do an excellent job at removing calluses.

- ◈ **Soak your feet.**
  A wonderful way to pamper your feet. Add Epsom salts or some peppermint oil.

- ◈ **Rub your own feet.**
  Alternatively, you can ask a loved one.

- ◈ **Give yourself the gift of a Reflexology Treatment.**
  Although this massage therapy focuses on the feet, it actually treats the whole body. The reason being that every body part is connected to the foot.

- ◈ **Remove calluses regularly.**
  This can be done in the shower with a pumice stone or by using a 'Ped Egg' to remove the dead skin.

◆ **Try massaging your own feet.**
While sitting or standing, roll your feet over a tennis or golf ball. Some areas may be tender, yet over time, they will release. You can also massage your own feet by rubbing some oil into your hands and lovingly let yourself be guided.

"The human foot is a masterpiece of engineering and a work of art."
~ Leonardo da Vinci

THE BODY AND THE ENVIRONMENT
where the outside meets your internal world.

There are numerous ways in which you can choose to take exquisite care of yourself and at the same time be responsible and mindful of the planet. The good news is both choices partner up to make an excellent team and one of the first places to begin is your home.

Paint

The very walls of your home may be the resident of toxins and other substances harmful to your health. Be mindful of safe building materials such as insulation, dry wall and paints. There is always a choice as to the type of paint or product you use, therefore choose brands that emit less odors, fumes and toxicity.

Mold

Mold can be silent and invisible, yet even more dangerous. There are different types, yet the most toxic is black in color. If your house, roof, basement or washing machine has ever leaked or flooded, beware. The mold can be growing behind walls, in the attic or under floors and its impact is a continuous attack to the immune system.

For those of you already sensitive to mold because of a history with Candida, it can be obvious when a room feels damp and mold- infested. Usually the signs are the space feels cold, damp, and dank and yields very little sunlight or ventilation. You may or may not be able to see the actual mould itself. Obviously, bathrooms are an issue considering the steam from the bath or shower. Also, pay attention to sprinklers causing water damage. Installing fans, opening windows, having the area checked by a professional and making repairs and adjustments where necessary, are all vital components to your health and well-being.

"Recently, I chose not to sleep in a lofty guestroom and crashed on a sofa instead, because the room felt so mold ridden." ~ Miranda

Ways To Keep A Mold Free Environment:

- Keep the room ventilated by opening a window.

- Use a fan if installed.

- Check for leaks around the seals of the bath and shower so water is not leaking into the walls or floor.

- Visually check for signs of mold in and around the shower or bath.

- Leaky sprinklers can also be a problem if the water is seeping into the foundation of the house.

The symptoms in the body that show you might be living in a damp, mold infested space are headaches, foggy headedness, sinus infections, Candida, yeast infections, fatigue or low energy, to name a few. Of course, some of these symptoms could have other causes, but it is certainly worth checking.

Gardens

The use of safe garden products protects you and your loved ones as well as your pets. The more you go back to what nature intended the better. Also, pay attention to what your gardener may be using.

Household Products

Be conscious to honor the use of safe household products for cleaning and the general maintenance of your home. These products are less expensive and protect you and the water supply when they are flushed down the drain. The toxins produced from the use of less environmentally conscious cleansers can be an irritation to the eyes, the respiratory system, the skin and the planet.

Keep Your Home Environment Safe

◆ Be aware of what your housekeeper may be using.

◆ Choose products that are cruelty-free and not tested on animals.

◆ There are many old-fashioned recipes for cleaning that work well such as vinegar, lemon and baking soda.

◆ Products from Mrs. Meyers are excellent.
  These formulas are safe and have a delightful array of scents.

◆ Search online for inventive and effective recipes and suggestions.

"After the recent purchase of a house I have been learning about the rather complicated world of septic tanks and cesspools. It seems these underground sewage systems are no different to the living organisms of our bodies. The rule of thumb is the tank needs to be fed with friendly bacteria in order to break down the waste and if anything toxic such as bleach or chemicals are released into it, the balance is destroyed. This will result in having to clean the tanks more often and possible sewage overflow! Therefore, I have become extremely conscious of what goes down the drains of my house. I know many of you are probably connected to the sewage mains, yet the same toxins are still being dumped somewhere on our precious planet." ~ Miranda

Heating And Air Conditioning

Here is a simple note regarding heating and cooling your home. Logically, every time you turn on these appliances, there is an effect on the environment. However, you might entertain the idea of not only saving on your utility bills, but also prevent drying out your skin, hair and respiratory system by using these machines as little as possible. As the utility companies continually encourage, a jacket or another layer of clothing in the winter can keep your heating bill down and encourages your desire to cuddle up to someone. Similarly, a cooling shower, a run in the sprinklers or ice cubes can often do the job of cooling you down in the summer.

Electronic Equipment

Do not negate the effects of electronic equipment in your environment. Be conscious to unplug or remove all electrical or cellular appliances from your bedroom, particularly while you are sleeping. Once again, what is good for you is good for the environment as many items plugged into your home do continue to use energy. Simply unplugging the toaster or the heater from the wall will save on energy consumption.

Carpets, Furniture And Linens

If you have ever walked into a room with newly laid carpet, you may have noticed the strong, chemical odor in the room. Many carpets outgas for the first few days after they are installed. The use of carpets or floor coverings made of natural fibers and materials prevents such occurrences. The same awareness can be applied to mattresses, pillows, bedding, towels, blankets and furniture. If you have made a decision to purchase items that are not made of natural materials, leave them outside for a few days or leave the windows open in the room to provide plenty of ventilation. This will alleviate the impact on you or your family.

Water Filters

Household water systems that filter or soften the water are better for your skin and thus your health. Many showerheads on the market filter the water on the spot and provide cleaner water in which to bathe. It is remarkable how your skin feels after showering or bathing in this water. The soap reacts differently on your skin and is often easier to wash off or you may find need you use a lot less.

"The environment is everything that isn't me."
~ Albert Einstein

Yet it is still the responsibility of each individual to honor and respect the surroundings of this natural world, which houses and supports every one of us.

COOKWARE

You are in which you cook.

The use of certain types of cookware is important to discuss, because depending on what the pan is made from, the material is absorbed into the food and then into your body. More and more information has been published about safe cookware and kitchenware, especially in light of its possible side effects on the body.

- **Avoid aluminum and non-stick Teflon products.**
  Pure stainless steel with aluminum fillings is acceptable if the instrument is in excellent condition. Scratches or dents in the outer surface may allow exposure to the aluminum insulation.

- **Use cast iron, enamel and stainless steel or glassware products.**

- **Check the materials used in these products.**
  Some cookware may be ninety percent of one material with a few hidden surprises. It is not worth endangering your health.

- **Use wooden chopping boards.**
  They naturally kill off bacteria.

- **Do not heat plastic as it can leach into the food.**

TRAVEL

Staying balanced and centered while going on a walkabout.

Whether you are traveling for business or pleasure, the more accustomed you become to honoring the needs of your body, the more you will realize that travel has its own unique set of circumstances and conditions. Recognizing the special considerations of your body when you are traveling will make for a successful business trip or a pleasurable vacation. There is nothing like planning the perfect ski vacation and then upon arrival, acquiring a good case of altitude sickness that keeps you off the slopes for a few days. The inside of the hotel room may be lovely, but this is not exactly what you had planned.

Here Are Some Tips For Successful Trips:

- **Hydrate.**
  Climate changes and flying require that the body be generously hydrated to feel its best. Remember to drink plenty of fluids before, during and after your trip.

- **Constipation is common during travel.**
  Water will help this condition, but also magnesium, Natural Calm or vitamin C work well.

- **Take probiotics and digestive enzymes.**
  Dietary practices usually take a beating while traveling. Sometimes you may eat too much or try unfamiliar or uncommonly rich foods. It is rare to maintain a similar diet to the one at home when you are experiencing different time zones, cultures or various eating conditions. Probiotics and digestive enzymes help rebalance the body and prevent food poisoning and parasites.

- **Eat the local yogurt or kefir.**
  This gives the body the friendly local bacteria of the region you are traveling in. This helps to support your immune system, aligns the body with the environment and can prevent food poisoning.

- **Sitting for long periods of time in an airplane, airport, train, car or other mode of transportation can affect the digestion.**
  Moving around and stretching are helpful.

- **Get up and walk around the plane.**
  It is crucial to move about every couple of hours. In addition, if you are drinking enough, having to go to the bathroom will take care of this.

- **Take a travel remedy. Examples are 'No Jetlag' or Arnica Montana.**
  The biorhythms of the body are upset as it crosses many time zones. Both these remedies aid in balancing the body during and after trip, especially long ones. It is a simple as sucking on a tasty little pill every couple of hours.

- **While flying, drink plenty of water.**

- **Do not consume alcohol during the flight.**
  If you feel that you need an alcoholic drink to calm your nerves or because you are afraid of flying, take Rescue Remedy instead. It will take the edge off your fear without dehydrating and harming the body.

- **Take Electrolytes while travelling.**
  They will rebalance your electrolytes and rehydrate you.

- **If you are traveling to another country, it is wise to check with your Doctor or Naturopath regarding the prevention or removal of parasites.**

- **Be conscious of the water you are consuming in foreign lands, including ice cubes and on raw food such as salads.**

- **Be sure to pack your own skin care products.**

- **Natural bug spray and sunscreen are crucial.**
  Choose a natural insect repellent that uses essential oils such as eucalyptus, lemongrass or citronella rather than deet or other chemical compounds.

- **Other natural remedies:**
  - ◊ Rescue Remedy ~ for stress and trauma.
  - ◊ Rescue Remedy Cream ~ for itching, bites or rashes.
  - ◊ Traumeel Cream ~ for bruises, bumps or aching muscles.
  - ◊ Essential Oils ~ for calming the nerves, baths, as insect repellent or to smell good!
  - ◊ Vitamin C ~ for constipation and immunity.
  - ◊ Natural Calm ~ for regular bowel movements and a good night's sleep.
  - ◊ Travel Ease and Sage Spray ~ these clear you and a room's energy field.
  - ◊ Incense ~ to invoke an uplifting atmosphere.

And always, a good book and your own pillow!

REVEAL MORE TRUTH

Luxuriate in self-care.

This time during 'Body Care' evokes the sensual and allows you to slip into the realms of luxurious pampering.

The good news is that it does not have to cost money. Just by filling a bathtub with salts, essential oils, lighting a candle and giving yourself some precious time is a gift you can always afford.

Take this time to incorporate the teachings from the last few teachings of 'The Foundational Trinity' and now weave in exquisite and loving self-care. The body is not to be ignored and as you pay attention to her, you will hear the messages and become in tune with her needs and desires. When you choose to be in partnership with this miraculous housing for your being, it is a win-win situation. Yet when you ignore her, your foundation and overall health will start to crumble.

INVITATIONS TO YOUR BODY CARE COMMITMENT:

- **Give yourself the gift of at least one body care treatment during this time.**
  This could be a massage, a facial or a treatment at a spa. If money does not allow, see if you can receive a foot or back rub from a friend or lover.

- **Once a week spend an hour or so pampering yourself.**
  Soak in a hot tub, which smells good. Do a facemask. Spend some time moisturizing your whole body. Lather your hair in olive oil or conditioner and leave it on for a few hours. Find your own way to love and honor your body.

- **Pay attention to any area of the body that is giving you a message. It could be an ache, a pain or tightness.**
  Consciously spend a few moments in silence and listen to your body's message. You can use the symbology information to help guide you, but your own intuition is always the best. It is your body after all.

◆ **Fill in the Self-Care Chart.**
The beauty of this chart is that it weaves 'The Foundational Trinity' together. It will lay out a strong foundation for the journey ahead, as you incorporate new ways of being into your life.

View this time as a way to express love to yourself fully. Your body will respond majestically and you will benefit by feeling beautiful, sensual, pampered and loved.

Give yourself this gift. With all my love and support,

Miranda

CHARTS, CHARTS, GLORIOUS CHARTS

*"She made a promise to herself
to hold her own well-being sacred."*
~ Quote

This Exquisite Self-Care Chart will bring a whole new level of awareness and consciousness to the foundation of your life. In addition, it will give you clarity beyond measure on what is working in your world and what is not.

◆ Please go to **www.MirandaJBarrett.com/resources/body-care** to print out more copies for yourself. Give yourself the gift of seeing your self-care needs clearly laid out in front of you.

◆ Fill out the **Exquisite Self-Care Chart** on a daily basis until you begin to see your sleep, healthy food, water and exercise patterns.

◆ Ask yourself the powerful question: Are your self-care activities nurturing and respecting your body, inside and out?

◆ Once you are clear about your basic self-care needs and see the importance of honoring this vital aspect of your life, make the necessary adjustments to lovingly replenish and nurture yourself.

*"Self-care is not about self-indulgence,
it's about self-preservation."*
~ Audrey Lorde

A DAILY PRACTICE
FOR EXQUISITE SELF-CARE

	MONDAY	TUESDAY	WEDNESDAY	THURSDAY	FRIDAY	SATURDAY	SUNDAY
NUTRITION Breakfast							
Lunch with vegetables							
Dinner with vegetables							
Snacks Healthy							
WATER How much?							
SLEEP How much?							
MOVEMENT What kind?							
For how long?							

This chart combines and synthesizes your relationship with
'The Foundational Trinity' of Sleep, Movement, and Nutrition.

Please go to
www.MirandaJBarrett.com/resources/body-care
to print out more copies for yourself.

ABOUT MIRANDA
A spirited guide and mentor.

Miranda is a passionate and devoted leader. Her loving and wise support will guide you on a transformational journey as her powerful teachings unveil the truth of who you are. Her gift is to offer potent tools, which inspire exquisite and beautiful self-care and empower you to live the fullest and most authentic life possible. As a mentor and guide, Miranda deeply walks her talk and is fearless about her own path of self-discovery, as she weaves the sacred into the mundane.

The simple, yet powerful premise offered by the mystic Rumi is the foundation of Miranda's philosophy and mission:

> *"Never give from the depths of your well,*
> *always give from your overflow."*

Miranda gives Council and Guidance for the Mind, Body and Spirit. With a background in Nutrition and Energy work, Miranda is the Creator of 'A Woman's Truth' and 'The Spirit of Energy', an Author, a Workshop and Retreat Leader, a Reiki Master and Yoga and Meditation teacher. Miranda studies under the guidance of her Beloved teachers Rod Stryker and Adyashanti.

To speak with or follow Miranda, please call or visit:

Phone: 626~798~6544
eMail: Info@MirandaJBarrett.com
Website: www.MirandaJBarrett.com
Facebook: Miranda J Barrett
Twitter: MirandaJBarrett

ABOUT HELENA

A visionary artist.

Helena Nelson-Reed is a visionary artist whose primary medium is watercolor. Born in Seattle, Washington, she was raised in Marin County and Napa Valley, California and today lives in Illinois. A largely self-taught artist whose educational emphasis and degree is in psychology, Nelson-Reed's primary focus is exploring the collective consciousness and the portrayal of archetypal imagery in the tradition of Carl Jung and Joseph Campbell. Rendered in luminous watercolor technique often described as ephemeral, Nelson-Reed's paintings are created in extraordinary detail, pushing the medium of watercolor past the usual limits. Her work may be found in private collections, book covers, magazines and cd covers. Nelson-Reed also has a line of jewelry, calendars and greeting cards.

Helena's Mission:

My images can be interpreted many ways, and for some will serve as portal to the mythic landscape. Descriptions providing background about each painting are available by request. Navigating and translating myth into contemporary wisdom is the traditional way of transmitting information though a shamanic and multi-cultural practice.

Myth, fairy, folk and spiritual lore describe divine beings and supernatural life forms arriving unbidden and disguised. In our earthly dimension, mortals often play similar roles in the lives of one another. Destinies and energies collide and interact, visible and invisible forces are at work. The mythic realms are timeless, offering insight and inspiration. While my paintings have a positive energy, many have roots in the shadows of life experience and human psyche; like the lotus blossom rooted in pond mud. For many, life is one challenge followed by the next, like beads on an endless string.

Take heart! Like goddess Inanna, one may navigate the underworld, move through dark places yet return to the realms of light battle scarred but wiser, richer for the experience. Read the ancient tales, the great mythic literature; draw strength, for they are repositories of wisdom.

Visit Helena's website for her art, purchase information and art to wear jewelry:

eMail: HNelsonReed@Gmail.com
Websites: www.HelenaNelsonReed.com
www.etsy.com/shop/HelenaNelsonReed
Blog: www.dancingdovestudio.blogspot.com
Facebook: MorningDove Design By Helena

MIRANDA'S WORLD

*Ways to stay connected
and aligned with your truth.*

BOOKS:

A Woman's Truth
A life truly worth living.

Priceless teachings reveal your transformational
journey ahead. Obstacles to self-care are explored
as clear and loving intentions are conceived.

The Grandeur of Sleep
Permission to rest.

Miraculous benefits are realized as the worlds of sleep,
relaxation and rejuvenation are explored and deeply honored.

Nourishing Nutrition
Reclaim your health and vitality.

Reap the bountiful rewards while eating as nature intended.
Claim your health and vitality with these simple,
yet powerful tools to nourish and heal your body.

Embodying Movement
Ground your whole being.

Restore balance in your life. Discover how to embrace
your whole being through the life-enhancing benefits of body movement.

Body Care
Cherish your body as a temple.

Learn to honor your extraordinary body
as a living temple and listen to the healing messages she whispers.

Feminine Power
Fully access your supreme birthright.

Welcome and reclaim this intrinsic privilege while living
in harmonious balance between the masculine and the feminine.

The Abundance Of Wealth
Receive the gifts of prosperity.

Understand the energy flow of prosperity and weave
the threads of abundance throughout the tapestry of your life.

Find Your Authentic Voice
The courage to express who you truly are.

Your greatest ally is born
when you courageously speak your truth and claim your unique power.

Loving Yourself
A love affair with the self.

As you become highly attuned to your own needs,
allow love to lead the way. Grant yourself permission
to honor and express your heart's truest desires.
Love yourself, no matter what.

Living A Spiritual Life
Ground your divine essence here on earth.

Discover what spirituality means to you, by consciously
living between the two worlds of the sacred and the mundane.

Service As A Way Of Life
Ignite the fire of love to truly be of service.

By utilizing the gems of exquisite self-care
on a daily basis and honoring your truth, your mission of service is born.

The Crowning Glory
Fully Rejoice in Being You.

A celebration overflowing with love,
blessings, grace and gratitude. Stand confident within
your own truth as your mind becomes of service to your heart.

The Food Of Life
The versatile vegetable.

More than just a cookbook,
a comprehensive guide for nourishing your life.

Reiki
The spirit of Energy.

An insightful guidebook full of wisdom
which introduces you to the potent and healing world of Reiki.

CARDS:

Inspiration Cards
A daily Spiritual Practice.

Sixty-Five cards with simple yet inspirational qualities
to live by and an insightful guidebook to lead the way.

CD'S:

The Grandeur of Sleep and Rejuvenating Rest

An ancient healing art of rest and relaxation.

Simple yet profound practices, which alleviate stress and tension allowing your mind, body and spirit to heal, restore and replenish.

TO ORDER PLEASE VISIT:

www.MirandaJBarrett.com
www.Amazon.com

*All books are available in printed or eBook form.

REFERRALS

Tried, trusted and tested.

The following are a list of people and products that come highly recommended. Feel free to call them or check out their websites.

For more references and referrals to support the exquisite self-care of your body, please visit Miranda's website at www.MirandaJBarrett.com/resources/body-care

Products:

The Golden Thread Store

All that you need to take exquisite care of the body
Phone: 626~798~6544
Web: www.MirandaJBarrett.com

Himalayan Institute

Supplies, Netti Pots, washes and tongue cleaners
Phone: 570~253~5551
Web: www.HimalayanInstitute.org

Plant Life

Exquisite bath salts
Phone: 888~708~7873
Web: www.PlantLife.com

Uriel Pharmacy

Exquisite lavender rose cream
Phone: 866~2858
Web: www.UrielPharmacy.com

Q Link

Small device worn on the body that aids in repelling electromagnetic energies
Phone: 800~246~2765
Web: www.Q-LinkProducts.com

Bio Pro

Electronic appliances to aid in reducing the impact of electric currents
Phone: 866~999~2747
Web: www.BioProTechnology.com

Resources:

Dr. Christian Northrup

Amazing books and wisdom on women's bodies and menopause
Web: www.drnorthrup.com

Joseph Mercola

Cutting edge information on health, wellness and nutrition
Phone: 877~985~2695
Web: www.Mercola.com

Body Ecology Diet

Donna Gates is a pioneer in the world of digestive health.
Phone: 800~511~2660
Web: www.BodyEcology.com

Skin Care Products:

Eminence

Natural skin care products
Phone: 888~747~6342
Web: www.EminenceOrganics.com

Derma e

Natural skin care products
Phone: 800~933~9344
Web: www.Dermae.com

DHC

Natural skin care products
Phone: 800~342~2273
Web: www.DHCcare.com

Dr. Hauschka

Natural skin care products
Phone: 800~247~9907
Web: www.DrHauschka.com

Epicuren

Natural skin care products
Phone: 800~235~1217
Web: www.Epicuren.com

TESTIMONIES
to 'A Woman's Truth' teachings.

"I heard about 'A Woman's Truth' from a friend. I had seen her transform before my very eyes and wanted to know her secret. I am now transforming before my own eyes and I love the process! What a gift I have given to myself."

Celeste ~ Talent Producer ~ Marina Del Rey, CA

"At first the idea of reading twelve books of 'A Woman's Truth' seemed like a big commitment. Yet I found myself really looking forward to reading each one. They were like a loving hand gently nudging me back to my center and ultimately it was all about making a commitment to me."

Mary Anne ~ Teacher ~ Santa Monica, CA

"It is so true that as a woman I am more radiant than I was before. I myself have made significant changes. I am able to speak my truth wherever I want to, which is always. I used to be concerned that others would not like me. Now I truly do not worry about it. Miraculous things happen all around me now and I notice them. Maybe they always did, but now I see them. Thank you Miranda for the gifts you have given me. They will allow me to give so much more to those around me."

Tricia ~ Principal ~ Altadena, CA

www.ingramcontent.com/pod-product-compliance
Lightning Source LLC
Chambersburg PA
CBHW080522110426

42742CB00017B/3203